‘kington

M ost people have an image of Cockington in their minds, be it from the souvenir plate hanging above Granny's mantelpiece or from a glance through a guide book of Devon. Those who have visited may know little about the place, except that it is a pretty thatched village sandwiched between Torquay and Paignton. After a browse through this book, you will hopefully see Cockington in a different light, having discovered the wealth of history and fascinating tales the area has to offer. The pages ahead are not intended to provide a complete history of Cockington; instead, I have tried to provide the concise version, which I hope will give an image of the real Cockington.

Cockington Village is situated in a valley, about two miles or so in length, which stretches from the Torbay Ring Road near Marldon to the sea at Livermead. The village itself is about a mile from the seafront. It is a pleasant surprise to most people to find a peaceful, rural valley within the urban district of Torbay. Cockington has survived the growth experienced by its neighbours, which is only too apparent in the modern houses teetering on the hill tops bordering the valley. The development stops there, however, leaving the 'rural showpiece' that half-a-million visitors come to enjoy every year.

So what are the origins of Cockington? Where did it all start? Well, some sort of settlement has existed here since long before the Norman Invasion of 1066. Cockington has existed from at least Saxon times; (that is, following the Romans but preceding the Normans for those who never remember these things). The place name, some say, means, 'The Settlement of the Red Meadow' and is partly Celtic, partly Anglo-Saxon. 'Coch' – red (Celtic); 'Ing' – meadow; and 'Ton' enclosure or settlement (Anglo-Saxon). Incidentally, for those wondering what 'red' has to do with the name, the answer is to be found in the soil of the area, which is a beautiful rusty red colour. This is a result of iron compounds breaking down in the sandstone rock below.

The whole of Devon was divided into 'Hundreds' in the late 800s by King Alfred. A Hundred contained either one hundred families or one hundred men suitable for war. Cockington was situated in the Hundred of Haytor. Quite why, we are unsure because Haytor was not even included in this area! Under Saxon law, meetings were held once a month. The meeting place for the Hundred of Haytor was near Stantor on the hills at the head of the valley, which provided a good look-out post for spotting warships.

All historical knowledge of Cockington before the end of the eleventh century comes from the Domesday Book of 1086. This was the result of a survey carried out on the orders of William the Conqueror to find out who owned each place in England. Most importantly, the survey was carried out to record the land resources of each settlement for taxation purposes. The Book tells us that in the time of Edward the Confessor (pre-Conquest), the Manor of Cockington belonged to a wealthy Saxon thane called Alric. Alric probably never lived for any length of time here as he also owned twenty-three other manors in Devon. In his time, it is thought that a manor house, estate and chapel existed and certainly, the Domesday excerpt implies that Cockington was a thriving place in the 1080s. It went something like this:

"William of Falaise has a Manor called Chochintona which Alric held on the day on which King Edward was alive and dead and it rendered geld for three hides. These can be ploughed by thirteen ploughs. Of this William has in demesne one hide and five ploughs, and the villeins have two hides and seven ploughs. There William has eighteen villeins and six bordars and fourteen serfs and one pack horse and eight head of cattle and 159 sheep and 42 goats and 50 acres of wood and 15 acres of meadow and 50 acres of pasture. This is worth 50 shillings and it was worth as much when William received it."

The excerpt tells us that Alric was displaced by William de Falaise after the Norman invasion. So what does all that mean? Well, William was to pay tax for three hides. A 'hide' was a homestead or farm holding, estimated roughly at 100 to 120 acres. The King took 6 shillings per hide per year in tax for the defence of the realm. This was a very old form of taxation even in those days, dating back to the Danish King Ethelred. Apparently 310 hides paid for one warship, while 8 hides allowed for a Jack (suit of armour) and a saddle. A 'plough' was about 50 acres. As to the people mentioned in the entry, serfs were almost slaves. Bordars (or cottagers) were occupiers of very small holdings, usually less than 5 acres. They were relatively free people but in return for this freedom they had to supply the Lord of the Manor with produce, often poultry and eggs. Villeins were small labouring farmers who enjoyed social and political rights and were free in return for perhaps one day's work for the Lord every so often.

So we have evidence of much happening in Cockington before Domesday. Now let's look at what happened after 1066 when the Battle of Hastings was fought. First, we will look at Cockington from the aspect of the owners of the estate. Later, we will find something out about the village and the people who lived and worked there.

It took a few years for the south-west of England to be taken by the Conqueror because the folk of Devon and Cornwall were resilient and did not welcome strangers perhaps! William held siege to Exeter, where the ex-King Harold's mother had taken refuge. By 1070, power in the West Country was fully established and the land was distributed among Norman friends and favourites. Cockington was given to William de Falaise, of whom little is known, except that like Alric, he was wealthy, owning many other places in Devon, such as Rattery and Harbertonford.

At an unknown date soon after Falaise's possession of Cockington, the Manor was passed in some way, either by grant or by marriage, to Martin Tours, Lord of Camoys in

Wales. His son, Robert FitzMartin, Lord of Dartington, gave Cockington, except for the church and some land, to his son Roger. It was Roger who, rather fancying the name 'Cockington', adopted it as the family surname. From that time, the de Cockingtons owned the estate for a period of over two hundred years, passing through seven or eight generations. For anyone wishing to study the family – a warning! Things start to get very confusing as most of the male descendants are called Sir Roger, with just two exceptions. Many of them represented the County of Devon in Parliament.

The last of the de Cockingtons was James, who was entitled the Sheriff of Devon in 1327. He was given Exeter Castle and the Port of Dartmouth by Edward III in the same year. The Port was quite lucrative at the time, yielding 100 shillings a year in customs. Sir James died in 1349, probably from the Black Death, which was prevalent in that year, causing the death of other family members. His wife, Joan, survived and inherited the Manor with a part passing to Sir Walter de Woodland. The entire estate passed to de Woodland on Joan's death in 1351. His main claim to fame was as Usher of the Chamber to the Black Prince. His wife, Katerina, inherited the estate twenty years later in 1371. It was in this year that the estate was passed to William Cary – probably by sale.

Along with his brother John, Sir William Cary represented Devon in Parliament in the 1360s. However, John who inherited the estate in 1381, is the more famous of the two. In 1386, he was made Lord Chief Baron of the Exchequer. All seemed fine until 1388, when Sir John was sentenced to death for supposed treason against King Richard II. The death sentence was not actually carried out; instead he was sent into exile. All his possessions were snatched, including Cockington, which was granted to John, Earl of Huntingdon, as Cary's children had lost the right of succession. Sir John was banished to Waterford in Ireland where he lived a meagre existence until his death in 1404. He was allowed £20 per year for maintenance and was forbidden to travel beyond two miles of the town. As far as Cockington went, the new occupant lost the manor for some reason and the new King, Henry IV, gave it to Sir Robert Chalons in 1400. As you can imagine, Sir John's son was not too happy about this and tried unsuccessfully to regain his father's estate. Restitution was finally granted by Henry V and by 1418, Sir Robert Cary was back in residence. The reason for this is said to be as a result of an armed combat, which Sir Robert won against a Knight of Aragon who came to England in 1413, challenging any man of rank to try his skill in 'mortal combat'.

The heroic Sir Robert's grandson, another William Cary, was attained by Parliamentary forces for joining the King's enemies in 1464 and was ordered to surrender or be charged with treason. As a result, Cockington was yet again removed from Cary hands. The lucky recipient this time was Sir Thomas Bourghchier. So what became of Sir William? He, along with other noblemen from the south-west, formed an army and fought the Battle of Tewkesbury, where most of them were treacherously beheaded on the battle field. As in the past, Cockington was restored to the Cary family some time later; the decapitated Sir William's son received the estate from Henry VII in 1485.

The most prominent member of the Cary dynasty was probably Sir George Cary, born in 1541 and the great grandson of Sir William. He was a distinguished lawyer and was fortunate to be a favourite of Queen Elizabeth. He showed particular courage in demobilising the Spanish Armada in 1588 for, along with Sir Edward Seymour of Torre Abbey, he raised and took command of the two South Devon regiments, a total of 1,600 men. Sir George was MP for Devon that year and was called to action from Dover where he had been co-ordinating defence. Following the defeat of the Armada, he and Sir John Gilbert of nearby Compton Castle, held 400 Spanish men in a barn at Torre Abbey, still to be seen today and known as the Spanish Barn. The prisoners had formed the crew of the Spanish galleon *Capitania*, which had been captured and brought to Torbay by the *Roebuck*; this was a ship belonging to Sir Walter Raleigh's fleet. Soon after, Sir George and Sir John fell out because Sir John employed 160 of the Spanish men to work in the grounds of Compton Castle, something of which Sir George did not approve!

In 1597, Sir George was made Knight and Lord Deputy of Ireland and then Treasurer of Wars. The latter was an honoured and high post with one of the best salaries in the country at £638.15s per year. Another position filled by Cary was one of the Lords of Her Majesty Queen Elizabeth I's Privy Council for Ireland. Sir George decided to retire in 1607 and returned to Cockington with his new wife (his first having died some time before) who was only fifteen! On retirement, he resolved to live the rest of his days 'to God and himself'. He thought that God would be pleased with him if he carried out some good deeds for charity, so purported to help the local poor by building seven almshouses. When completed, the fortunate souls that were housed were given one shilling a week and new clothes at Christmas. The deed that Sir George signed declared that all future Lords of Cockington Manor must nominate new occupants for the almshouses when one became vacant, who must be the poorest citizens in the parish. The houses were initially constructed close to Cockington Court, but were later demolished and rebuilt further away from the house, which we shall find out about later.

Sir George died eight years later in 1615 but his legacy lived on. A report issued by the Charity Commissioners on Almshouses in 1905 states that the almshouses were then occupied by six women and one man. Each was receiving one shilling per week plus at Christmas, an equal share of "44 yards of blue frieze, 28 yards of dowlas, 7 yards of canvas and 1 pound of thread..." Cary is buried in a vault inside Cockington Church as requested in his will.

The last Cary to own Cockington was Sir Henry, the son of Sir George's nephew. The story of Sir Henry is similar to that of his predecessors who forfeited the estate. Henry served as Sheriff of Devon in 1638 and was knighted in 1644 by Charles I. This was because he had raised a regiment in support of the King, being a staunch Royalist supporter. Two years later, Sir Henry was forced to surrender at Kingswear Castle. Although he was pardoned, he was heavily fined and could not afford to keep Cockington estate. The sale took place in 1654, which marks the beginning of the Mallock family in Cockington. Poor old Sir Henry emigrated to America with his family. Today, his American descendants come to Cockington in order to trace their ancestry. A branch of the Cary family later owned the mansion and grounds at Torre Abbey until the 1930s when it was sold to the local authority .

Roger Mallock was a wealthy goldsmith from Exeter who originated from a well-established family from Axmouth in East Devon. His family were to own Cockington for nearly three hundred years, like the Carys. To make matters difficult, a similarity with the earlier de Cockingtons is that the men in the Mallock family seem to have the same names, either Rawlyn or Roger! Roger's son, surprisingly enough called Rawlyn (the first), made a great number of changes to Cockington Estate from 1659. In fact the man-made landscape features we see today were largely shaped by Rawlyn's hand. He rebuilt the mansion house, Cockington Court, which was completed in 1679. Before this, the house was much smaller and was probably thatched. He also created extensive gardens and walled off an area to form a rabbit warren. In career terms, Rawlyn was a Whig in Parliament. In 1688, when William of Orange arrived at Brixham, he was one of the small band of gentlemen to greet him.

A feature of the Mallock family tree seems to be that some Lords of the Manor died without an heir. Although the Estate was kept in the family, the line of accession is not generally one of simple father to son. For instance, Rawlyn's son died unmarried and the Estate was passed to another Rawlyn, who appears to be a cousin. Cousin Rawlyn gained the reputation of abetting the smuggling cause, allowing booty to be stored in his barns.

A letter written by Rawlyn (the fourth) in 1753 gives us a good picture of what Cockington was like at that time:

"There is a good ancient built house fitt for any gentleman on the Barton of Cockington also on the same a wood of 30 acres well stocked with a great number of oak trees and the more valuable because but a mile or two from the sea. The deer park in the Barton of Cockington comprises of 100 acres. It is stocked with 120 deer which may be purchased with the estate, also there are seven fish ponds well stocked with carp and trout. There is a rabbit warren on this Barton with walls all round for the space of two miles, which walls cost about £200 and there is a pleasure house on the top of the warren that has a fine prospect of all Torbay only at a mile distant."

Sounds idyllic but things were to change under a notable member of the family, the Reverend Roger, who dramatically changed the appearance of Cockington. He was Squire of Cockington for sixty years (1786–1846) from the age of fourteen. He abandoned the deer park, turning the land over to arable farms, which could be rented to local farmers for a higher profit. However, the most significant alteration was to Cockington Court. The house was modified in 1820, some say for the worse, by removing the gables of the two wings and reducing the height of the second storey, the windows of which became skylights. Other windows were blocked or boarded over. It is believed that this was done because the Reverend could not afford to pay window tax, which was in force at the time. The window tax was introduced in 1696 and it was intended to help pay

for a new coinage. All house owners with more than six windows were liable for payment until 1851 when it was abolished. By reducing the number of windows, the Reverend would have lessened his tax bill substantially! He also added the columnar pillars to either side of the front entrance. A curious piece of engineering shows that these must have previously been used elsewhere, as the centre portions of the pillars have been cut out and reversed. On the reverse side is the Cary coat of arms! W.H. Mallock, a later inhabitant of the Court, elaborates on the changes as follows:

"He…destroyed the forecourt of his house and a range of antique offices, considerably reducing…the size of the main building by depriving it of its top storey and substituting a dwarfish parapet for what had once been its eight gables."

W.H. Mallock also tells us that the inside of the house was ruined to a greater extent by the Reverend Roger:

"A hall with minstrels gallery was turned by him into several rooms as commonplace as it is possible to imagine. Indeed little of special interest survived him…"

This 'tidying-up' process continued in the Court Grounds. A number of buildings had existed in front of the house as well as the old almshouses, which were close by. These were all cleared, resulting in a clear view from the mansion in about 1820. Most of these buildings were around one hundred years old. The almshouses were of course rebuilt in the village.

By the mid-1830s, Cockington was becoming a suburb of Torquay. The new road along the seafront enabled visitors to stroll into Mallock territory. The Reverend was none too happy about his privacy being invaded, so became involved in some road diversions. In 1838, the lane from the seafront road to Cockington was diverted so it did not enter the Mallock park and a lodge house was built to clearly establish the frontier!

In 1900, Captain, later Major, Charles Herbert Mallock inherited the Estate. He was an officer in the Royal Artillery until 1906 when he returned to live in Cockington with his bride. His homecoming was marked, by the local folk, with festivities including a band,

6

fireworks and fairy lights festooning the path from Higher Lodge to Cockington Court! At the outbreak of war in 1914, C.H. Mallock rejoined his regiment. He saw much active service and was awarded the D.S.O. However, he was killed by German mustard gas in 1917 in Ypres, where he is buried. There is a memorial to him in Cockington Church. His son and heir was too young to inherit the Estate at ten years of age, so it was leased to a J.H. Charlesworth for twelve years. The heir, who was to be the last private owner of the Court, took residence in 1928.

Like his great grandfather, Richard Herbert Mallock disliked visitors in his grounds. By this time, Cockington was a popular haunt for tourists, with its picturesque cottages and rural atmosphere, a distinct contrast to the hustle and bustle of Torquay. However, the new Lord of the Manor rather overstepped the line and, at the same time, highlighted a strange fact about Cockington Church. R.H. (as we shall call him for brevity's sake) erected a gate at the main entrance to the Court Grounds, which was kept locked. All very well, but as those who have visited will know, Cockington Parish Church is situated in the grounds next to the manor house. The strange truth is that although the Church owns the building, it owns no land around it. So no-one could get to Church! Obviously the Church was not going to put up with this and took the case to the Chancery Division of the High Court of Justice. An order was issued which allowed right of access to services and pedestrians between 9.00 a.m. and 6.30 p.m. daily. However, the Mallock era in Cockington was nearing an end for in 1932, R.H. sold the entire estate.

Initially, Cockington was bought as a whole by Torbay Council and administered by the Cockington Trust. At the end of the Second World War, the Council could no longer afford to maintain the buildings in the village, so in 1946 put it up for auction. Strangely enough, the Prudential Assurance Company were the lucky buyers. The Auctioneer commented: "I know that all the directors are very fond of it. They know Cockington well and I am certain that they will do nothing…that will interfere with its beauties."

As well as about 300 acres of land, Cockington Court was retained by the local authority. The house has been used for a variety of things since 1932. For a while it was the home of Lord Rothermere's art collection, later an ice cream factory and a home for the Parks Department of the Council. The beginning of the 1990s saw a new and more suitable use for the old manor: the home of the Devon Rural Skills Trust. The Court underwent large-scale renovations and opened as a craft centre where the public could watch craftspeople at work. Skills on show

ranged from cottage industry crafts such as patchwork to traditional hurdle fences.

So we now know something of the history of Cockington Court and its inhabitants. But what of the surrounding countryside and the village which is so well known? Let us now embark on a tour around Cockington Valley. Cockington Village enjoys world-wide fame for its thatched cottages, a few of which are now gift shops. Underneath however, a great deal of history is concealed. Surprising though it may seem, some visitors believe that Cockington is an unauthentic 'model village' built by the Prudential in recent years. Far from it; most of the buildings are at least three hundred years old!

Visitors often ask how many people actually live in the village. In 1086, approximately 200 people lived here and by 1659 the figure had risen to 360. In 1801 the number dropped to 294 and by 1871, dropped even more, to 188. In the 1990s the figure dropped to about 50 residents.

Most of the villagers were involved in either agriculture or fishing. Cockington labourers, I am told, always had a good reputation for hard work, although like most were poorly paid. Fishing seems to have been a major industry in the village. From Bailiffs records from the 1400s, we can see that the Carys employed fishermen and often bought nets and such like. Boats were launched at Livermead where salt cellars for preserving fish were kept as well.

The most famous aspect of the village itself must be its thatched roofs. Thatching was the traditional method of roofing houses until the advent of slates and tiles in the eighteenth century. Most labourers cottages were built of cob (a mixture of earth and straw) and thatched, as this was then a cheap method of construction. The advantage of a thatched roof is that it is warmer in the winter and cooler in the summer. The cottages in Cockington today are generally thatched with water reed with the ridges made from Devon wheat reed. In the past, the roofs would have been wheat reed entirely, which would have been grown locally. Today, most water reed is brought from Eastern Europe. The main supplier used to be Norfolk but, due to conservation measures, supply has decreased. Ridges take the most wear and need replacing on average every seven years. The actual roof can last up to 60 years, depending on the quality of reed used.

The focal point of the village is probably the forge, which is one of the great tourist attractions of Devon. A 1935 brochure comments that:

"The feature of surpassing interest and by which the name of Cockington is best known today is its blacksmith's forge, which is almost as famous...as its sister at Gretna Green."

Characterised by its timber props supporting the neat thatch, the forge is said to date back to the fourteenth century. The first available reference to a blacksmith working at

the forge is in 1615, when Mr Davey was the smith. His apprentice Anthony Hopping later married Davey's daughter, Grace. During the twentieth century, made and sold by the farrier were miniature horseshoes, which were immensely popular with visitors. Another popular custom associated with the building was that visitors used to leave card or pieces of paper with their names and addresses on, which were lodged into the thatched roof. This was eventually stopped, being deemed a fire risk!

The clink of the blacksmith's tools was heard up until 1971 when the forge closed due to a diminishing workload. At this time, the same blacksmith had been working there since the late 1940s. The craft of shoeing horses is thought to have arrived in Britain with the Normans. The horses that are kept in Cockington today, for providing cart rides for visitors, are served by a mobile farrier.

Traditionally, the home of the village blacksmith was 'Rose Cottage'. The cottage and its grounds now contain a wishing-well, stocks and, during the summer, a pianist playing on the bandstand! You may well laugh as you take a picture of a member of your family locked in the stocks, but once they formed part of the plethora of punishments available for use. Apparently there was a pond and ducking stool outside the forge, where gossiping women were given a dip. Rather more serious than stocks and ducking stools were the pit and gallows. The pit was a hole in the ground filled with water where female offenders were drowned. The gallows were reserved for the men. They were sited on the hills to the north of Cockington, now termed 'Gallows Gate' roundabout on the Torbay Ring Road. Few were sent to the gallows, however; fines were the most common form of penalty. Since Norman times, the Lord of the Manor had the power to administer capital punishment. Held regularly were the Court Leet and the Court Baron. The Court Leet allowed offenders to be sentenced. Interestingly enough, offences recorded in the Court Rolls include a landlord letting someone get drunk, eaves dropping, cutting trees down without permission and trespass. All inhabitants, offenders or not, had to appear before a jury twice a year and their good behaviour had to be vouched for. The Court Baron dealt with problems between the Lord of the Manor and his tenants and between tenants themselves.

To return to more pleasant matters, let us go back to Rose Cottage. There is some debate as to how old this building is. Some say sixteenth century, others firmly believe it is much older. The reason for this is that during floor excavations in 1955, an old pilgrims bottle was found, possibly dating back to the thirteenth century. The cottage was the birthplace of Robert Sweet, the renowned horticulturalist. He was born in 1782 to William and Mary Sweet. After a few years working as a gardener and nurseryman in Bristol and London, Sweet was employed by Messrs Colvill in London. Soon after in 1824, he was accused of receiving a box of plants known to be stolen from the Royal Gardens at Kew. He was sent to trial at the Old Bailey, but was acquitted. From 1826, while living in Fulham and later Chelsea, he wrote a number of books of a botanical nature, notably *The Botanical Cultivator* and *The British Flower Garden*. He died in 1835.

Rose Cottage has seen use as a post office and village store and between 1933 and 1939 also was used by handloom weavers. In the latter year, the weavers moved across the road to what used to be the old 'Home Farm' and is now 'The Weavers Cottage'. The old Home Farm was thought to be attached to Alric's Saxon manor and was a working farm until 1939. The Weavers Cottage was once the farmhouse and the ruins behind the cottage were the farm buildings. Some parts of these ruins are thought to be Saxon in origin. The last tenants to work the farm were the Denbows who moved there from Staverton in 1920. In 1939, the farm itself moved to another site in Cockington Lane and was again called

'Home Farm'. The mainstay of the farm was dairying and beef production. The Denbows kept a herd of South Devon Cattle. Aptly named 'Cockington General' was a champion bull nurtured by the Denbows and he won top prizes at the Devon County Show over a number of years. The farm is no longer in existence since the death of the last Denbow farmer in the 1970s.

Next to The Weavers Cottage is the Mill House. The Mill was an integral part of the original Home Farm and is said to have been constructed in 1435. It ceased operations just after the end of the Second World War. Incidentally, during the war, the Cockington Home Guard stored its equipment in what is now the kitchen. The Mill, operated by a water-wheel, produced flour and provided power to run machines for sawing timber, threshing and grinding corn and combing reed for thatching. The water-wheel that you see today was installed in 1878 and built by a firm in Newton Abbot. It was restored in 1992 after having been out of use for about ten years following a gruesome accident involving a drunkard, so I am told! Water to power the wheel is stored in the Mill Pond also recently restored. Grain produced by the Mill was once stored in the Granary, which later served as a stable to Home Farm and today is a Gift shop. This building looks old but was actually reconstructed in 1968 after a devastating fire. Before that, it had lain derelict from the 1930s and was restored in 1958.

Back to the centre of the village, fifteenth century 'Court Cottage' is a Devon longhouse, a characteristic building in this part of the West Country. Although the largest concentration are to be found on Dartmoor, Cockington has its fair share too. The layout of a longhouse was such that livestock could be accommodated under the same roof as the farmer's living quarters. The animals were kept in stalls with a central drain running down the floor, so all the waste collected and drained out of the building. Longhouses usually slope slightly downhill, with the livestock part (called a 'shippon') at the lowest level. Court Cottage retains the central drain under the new floor of the gift shop. The cottage has seen a variety of uses over the years. It was once a home for various branches of the Mallock family, a Court house for the village and also in later times the Cockington

Estate Office. Until 1892, the front part of the building, now the shop, was the village school. Mrs Doney was the school mistress and she lived with her family in Lower Lodge built by the Reverend Roger Mallock. The footpath that crosses the Lodge, called Old Paignton Road, is known locally as Doney's Lane.

'Higher Cottage', near the main entrance to the Court Grounds, is also a longhouse. The shippon has not been converted into separate rooms, as is the case with other such houses, and could still be used as livestock accommodation if so desired.

'Lower Lodge' is not the only lodgehouse in the village. At the main entrance to the Court Grounds is 'Higher Lodge'. A building has existed on this site since the 1400s but a fire destroyed the original building and the 'new' lodge was built in 1710 to a new design. The roof was made to overshoot and is carried on tree trunks, giving a truly countrified impression. Pevsner, the acknowledged building critic, describes the picturesque lodge as so: *"...its rustic verandah of tree trunks, supporting the thatched roof, and Gothic windows with straight-sided heads instead of arches."*

Turning towards the sea, eastward down Cockington Lane, is Lanscombe House Hotel, the Dower house to Cockington Court. A tannery once operated here until the mid-1800s. The buildings were destroyed by fire in 1881.

The acclaimed architect Sir Edwin Lutyens is usually associated with grand buildings and memorials, such as Liverpool Cathedral and the Viceroy's House at New Delhi. However, did you know that he designed the village pub – 'The Drum Inn'? The Inn was completed and opened in 1936. It was originally to be named 'The Forge Inn' but was renamed after a poem written by Laurence Whistler given to Lutyens who in turn presented the poem to the owners of the establishment. The poem is engraved on glass and can be viewed inside the pub today.

The Drum Inn formed part of an aggrandizement plan for Cockington. Lutyens was asked by the Cockington Trust to 'redesign' the village in the 1920s. Plans were drawn up and included the construction of large new houses and shops in keeping with the old buildings centred around a village green. The Inn was the only part of the plan to come to fruition. The Drum itself was intended to be larger. The bricks that face the building were made specially to Lutyen's requirements. The upper part of the building is lime plastered and lime washed. The thatch is truly the crowning glory. The enormous chimney stacks are very similar in proportion to another of Lutyen's creations – the Cenotaph in London's Mall. Internally, nothing was spared and all fittings were architect designed. Since then, changes have been made inside, which today bears little resemblance to the original layout. In fact, if anything, today's interior is more rustic: Lutyen's design was quite modern. During the Second World War, the headquarters of the village Home Guard was in the cellars of The Drum. This was a good choice of location as the cellars are built of concrete and steel and are lined with asphalt. I am sure there were no problems in attendance – lucky fellows!

To the north of The Drum stand the seven almshouses mentioned previously. Today, the cottages are occupied by the oldest people in Cockington, still continuing the precedent set by old Sir George Cary. When a house becomes available, it is offered to the elderly person who has lived in Cockington for the longest time.

We have looked at the history of Cockington Court and village. Now it is time to put on the wellies and explore the surrounding countryside to find out about some of the landscape features we see on a walk around the valley today. To the north of Cockington Court, the valley was once an extensive area of orchards. Apples were grown to produce Cockington's own brand of cider and was once a major industry here. In fact, apples were still commercially grown well into the 1970s by the Denbows but they were taken elsewhere by the sackload to be made into cider. From Bailiffs records from the 1400s, we can see that the Carys were concerned with cider making. For example, in 1461, two large wooden barrels "for holding the lady's cider" were purchased for 2s.4d. These barrels were called pipes, each one holding about 105 gallons. The records show that in the same year, people were paid to collect and press apples for cider making. Until the 1940s, there was a pound house at the rear of Cockington Court where apples were pressed. A horse walked round and round the pound house, attached to a central pole, providing power to turn a wheel that drove the cider mill. Stone rollers crushed the apples, which went into a tank. The crushed apples were then put in hair cloth and placed in a press. Men worked the press to produce rough apple juice, which was allowed to ferment for a few days then left to mature for a few weeks. Waste apple pulp was fed to pigs.

Joan Lang in her book *Old Cockington* (1971) reports on a questionnaire issued to every parish in 1757, which gives us a good idea of the cider making activities in the valley. It showed that there were many orchards and that Bitter Sweets, Portugees, Hempton Bearers, Red Streaks, Pear Mains and Mediates were grown. Three or four hundred hogsheads of rough and sweet cider were produced yearly (a hogshead, by the way, is a small barrel holding about 52 gallons of cider).

A feature of the valley mentioned earlier is the rabbit warren, created by Rawlyn Mallock (the first) way back in the 1600s. The warren at Cockington was a man-made breeding ground for rabbits. The warren itself no longer exists and is now part of Manscombe Plantation, but the walls, which extend for about two miles, are still standing in places and have undergone restoration. Rabbits were brought to England from France in the twelfth century. They were weak creatures, unable to dig their own burrows, so artificial ones had to be made for them. Landowners valued the rabbit for meat and strictly protected the species from poaching. The warren was let to a tenant, the first of whom was Peter Parnell in 1659. The tenant could have the rabbits, but had to keep up the maintenance of the walls and paid £22 per year in rent. Later, in Victorian times, a gamekeeper was employed to rear pheasants in the woods, which was a profitable business. The gamekeeper lived in what is now known as the 'Gamekeeper's Cottage', at the top end of the Lakes. The building you see now is a reconstruction of the original, which was burned down by vandals in 1990. The upper part of the cottage has a wooden slatted gable, which was utilised for hanging game. The gamekeeper must have been fond of animals, for apparently, he shared the lower floor with his pigs! The last gamekeeper to live here was in 1936. The original building was thought to be sixteenth century, probably once a farmhouse.

Dare if you will venture into Manscombe Woods as the name 'Manscombe', some say, means 'evil valley'! Once, when poaching was a problem on the estate grounds, the woods contained man traps to catch the offenders. Doubtless, the evil valley lived up to its name. Robber's Lane cuts diagonally through the woods. This route was used by smugglers bringing their loot to Warren Barn. This avoided the village and was a direct route from the coast at Paignton. Warren Barn, restored in 1994, is a listed building described as a linhay. A linhay is a two storey open-fronted barn; hay was stored on the upper floor (probably along with the smugglers booty!), while livestock were housed on the ground floor.

At the foot of the wooded slopes lie the three lakes. Although there have been fish-ponds in Cockington since time immemorial, the lakes you see today have been created by the Borough Council, which owns and maintains all of the parkland. They are based on the ornamental ponds created in 1659. The lakes are particularly spectacular in spring-time when the towering rhododendrons, first planted by Rawlyn Mallock, are in flower. Long before this, when the monks of Torre Abbey had an interest in Cockington land (which we will find out later), fish ponds were probably created by order of the Abbey to provide trout and carp.

Bewhay Lane is an ancient trackway, which starts close to the Almshouses and leads towards Marldon. The lane is heavily sunken into the hill from hundreds of years of horses hooves, cart-wheels and footsteps. Others believe the lane was cut especially deep by robbers who could pounce on victims from above! The name 'Bewhay' is AngloSaxon and means 'above the hedge'. Today, it is worth walking up the stony track to the ridge

Cockington

beyond in order to obtain magnificent views over Cockington Valley to the sea beyond and the seven hills upon which Torquay is built. From this angle, it is possible to imagine what the area was like many moons ago before settlement took place in Torbay. Remember also when you walk Bewhay Lane that in olden days this used to be one of the main roads in the area!

Cockington Village is set in some beautiful countryside. The lands belonging to the old Lords of Cockington once extended a great deal further. Richard Mallock sold large areas of land in 1900 in neighbouring Chelston and Livermead, but fought to keep Cockington Valley free of development. His intentions were probably selfish in that he wanted to retain the area as a retreat for his own family, but the results have benefited everyone who visits the valley. The release of land for urban development eventually led to most of the farms in the area becoming unviable and now the Borough Council owns most of the farmland (about 300 acres in all), renting fields to local people who keep mainly horses, but also cattle and sheep. In 1990, the Valley was given Country Park status with the idea of achieving the following aims: to farm the land sensitively; to conserve wildlife; to help visitors understand and enjoy what they have come to see; and finally to ensure that Cockington remains alive as a working community. So far, a great deal of work has been carried out in the valley concerning the restoration of old landscape features in which the Devon Rural Skills Trust has played a key role. Stone walls have been patched up and reconstructed in a traditional way, some hedges have been steeped in order to keep them neat and stockproof, the orchards have been revitalised and many new footpaths have been created allowing visitors to explore this wonderful area.

We have looked at everything in Cockington except for one very important building. Last, but by no means least, one of the most well visited places in Cockington must be the Parish Church of St George and St Mary. Although it is thought that a chapel has existed on the same site since Saxon times, the oldest part of the church that we can see today is the tower, constructed between 1210 and 1230. In 1113, the Lord of Cockington Manor – Robert FitzMartin – gave the chapel to St Dogmaels Abbey on the Welsh Coast, which he had founded. For the next ninety years, the monks of St Dogmaels were in charge of services at Cockington and in return received the tithes and produce from the land. In 1196, Torre Abbey, just over a mile away, was founded.

A few years later, the monks took over the role that St Dogmaels had played. In the tower is a room with a fireplace and toilet facility, which was probably an office for a Canon from Torre. The chapel was enlarged in the thirteenth century and then again in the fourteenth century by the monks. The fourteenth century extension was made in order to accommodate a new chapel devoted to William and Johanna de Cockington who had supplied the Abbey with water by diverting a stream. The monks were so grateful that they proposed to hold mass every Wednesday to pray for the repose of the couple's souls when they died. The service continued every week until the 1500s. However, it was resurrected in 1988 with a service held every Wednesday at midday.

This arrangement with Torre Abbey lasted until the dreadful year of 1539. The accession of King Henry VIII to the throne caused a great deal of change to all churches in England, including Cockington. King Henry wanted to reform religious thinking in England and was cynical about the way monasteries were run. The Reformation brought the Dissolution of the Monasteries, resulting in the demolition of the buildings and the redistribution of monastic lands. In 1539, Torre Abbey was taken. The chapel in Cockington was stripped of its ornamentation and the Latin mass was forbidden and replaced by an English service.

After a relatively stable period for the church, the reign of Cromwell from 1649 to 1660 led to the final destruction of any remaining church decoration. At Cockington, the stained glass windows were smashed and the building whitewashed. Although bell-ringing was forbidden, a new bell was cast at Cockington in 1653, which is now on show inside the church.

The next important date in the history of Cockington church is 1881 when Cockington became independent from Torre Church and became a parish in its own right. From then

on a huge programme of restoration was undertaken including new bells, leaded windows and the rood screen. However, as if the church had not suffered enough, two German bombs landed close to the building in 1943, smashing some stained glass windows. The crater can still be seen today in an adjacent field to the south of the church. The roof was also partially ruined, exposing the dreaded death watch beetle that had been gnawing away at the timbers! A new roof ensued as well as new windows.

A striking feature of the church is that it has no graveyard. This illustrates that a chapel was provided by the owner of the Manor for his own use at some time. In fact, the only graves you will see are the three under the large beech tree between the church and Cockington Court. They are the graves of three beloved dogs belonging to the gamekeeper in the early 1900s! So where were Cockington people buried? Well, under some flower beds near the church are the remains of a mosaic path that was discovered by some workmen in the 1930s. This path is now known as the start of the 'Funeral Path' and leads to Bewhay Lane, over the hills to Marldon beyond. Although not based on any historical fact, could it be possible that burials took place at Marldon Churchyard? It seems unlikely as when someone was to be buried, the cortege would have had to make quite a trek. A more gruesome thought is that Cockington did once have a graveyard, but that it was disposed of during the Reverend Roger's 'clean-up'! Who knows?